# THE POETRY
# OF PEACE

# THE POETRY OF PEACE

Edited by David Krieger

Foreword by Terry Tempest Williams

A Robert Bason Book
Published by Capra Press
815 De La Vina Street
Santa Barbara, CA   93101
www.caprapress.com

Cover by Keith Puccinelli; book design by Kathleen Baushke
Body type is Minion.


Library of Congress Cataloging-in-Publication Data

The poetry of peace / edited by David Krieger; foreword by Terry
Tempest Williams.
    p. cm.
    ISBN 0-9722503-9-5 (trade pbk.) — ISBN 1-59266-000-2 (hardcover
numbered) — ISBN 1-59266-001-0 (hardcover lettered)
    1.Peace—Poetry.   2. Peace movements—Poetry.   3 American poetry.
I. Krieger, David.
PS595.P43    P64    2002
811'.6080358—dc21

                                                        2002013048

Edition: 10   9   8   7   6   5   4   3   2   1

First Edition

Courage! Stand up and stretch to that sky!
In that sky (which is part gray slush) rediscover
our innocent air colored blue by our sun
and the wink of a star, invisible, far.

—Barbara Mandigo Kelly

# Acknowledgments

This book would not have been possible without the creative efforts of poets of all ages from throughout the world who have participated in the Nuclear Age Peace Foundation's Barbara Mandigo Peace Poetry Awards. We thank each of these poets for sharing their talents and providing their insights into peace and the human spirit.

Nor would this book have been possible without the countless dedicated members and friends of the Nuclear Age Peace Foundation, whose generous support makes projects such as the poetry awards possible.

Judging a poetry contest is a difficult task, and we have been fortunate to have a wonderful group of talented poets volunteer their time to accomplishing this task. They have each contributed a poem to this volume. Descriptions of the judges may be found in the "About" section of the book.

Special thanks to Terry Tempest Williams, one of the most talented and perceptive writers on our planet, for providing the Foreword to this volume. Deep appreciation also to Frank K. Kelly, one of our Earth's wise elders and a great spirit, who contributed the essay on Barbara Mandigo Kelly, who was his wife for 54 years and the woman for whom the awards are named. Frank's original article appeared in *Art for the Soul's Sake*, a book edited and published by Nancee Cline in Santa Barbara in 2001.

Special thanks are also due to the chair of the Foundation's Poetry Committee, Perie Longo, along with Board members Ilene Pritikin and Selma Rubin, who reviewed the manuscript and offered helpful suggestions.

Kathleen Baushke did her usual high-quality job of setting the type for the volume with patience, skill and good humor. Keith Pucinnelli, a tremendously talented graphic artist, provided the cover design.

The Foundation's staff members helped in many ways in making the poetry contest run smoothly. Carah Ong deserves special mention for her work in preparing the poems for publication.

Thanks, finally, to Bob Bason at Capra Press for believing in this project and to Rich Barre, the Capra editor who oversaw the project with care and professionalism.

*To all who believe in peace*
*and pursue it with poetry in their hearts.*

# *Peace Is. . .*

More than the absence of war

The global architecture of human decency

Putting the planet ahead of profit

Basic security for all

Freedom from oppression

Recognition of human dignity—
    *theirs* as well as *ours*

Everyone's inalienable right

Living gently on the Earth

The courage of nonviolence

A process, not an end

A thousand cranes in flight

A gift to children everywhere


— David Krieger

# Contents

## PART III — DREAMS AND FEARS

## PART IV — MAGIC AND WONDER

## PART V—LESSONS

## PART VI—ABOUTS

## PART VII—INDEXES

# FOREWORD

# *A Picture of Peace*

### By Terry Tempest Williams

On my desk sits a photograph of my niece, Diane. She is standing in front of a cotton sheet painted red with a large white star to the side and the word "COURAGE" written in blue across the homemade banner. This banner was thumbtacked to a wooden partition hastily erected in front of Ground Zero. We had made a pilgrimage from Salt Lake City, Utah, to Manhattan. Diane wanted to see for herself the hole in America's heart. Her face is stoic. Her eyebrows are raised. She is wearing black. She is eleven years old, soon to be twelve. The date was December 7, 2001.

Pearl Harbor comes to mind, though the similarities between September 11 and "the day of infamy" bear little historical reference. Hiroshima and Nagasaki come to mind, only because these are days of deep collective sorrow—days, moments in history when civility was shattered, lives were lost, and a pause gathered from the ground up like smoke, begging us to reconsider the relationship between power and peace.

Diane picked up a black magic marker and wrote her name on the sheet, offering the words "God Bless America" alongside hundreds of other signatures. She handed me the pen and I wrote my own sentiments, something about "Do we have the strength to see this wave of destruction as a wave of renewal?" I don't think I signed my name.

We could see past the scaffolding to the last remaining facade of the World Trade Center, which had become a standing memorial to those who had died. We watched the firemen work among the rubble, appearing like yellow jackets swarming around carrion. We stepped aside as an ambulance entered the site. Another body had been found.

Walking back toward SoHo, we stopped to see a special exhibit honoring 9.11 called "Here is New York: A Democracy of Photographs." Thousands of images hung on white walls, others were clothes-pinned to wires strung across the room. These were photographs taken by professionals and amateurs, tourists and residents, children and adults, anyone who had taken a picture and had a desire to share. You were invited to pick an image that spoke to you. The photograph would be sent to your home. Your contribution of twenty-five dollars would go to the Children's Fund of September 11.

I watched Diane walk up one side of the room and down the other. I wondered which photograph she would choose. I thought about which image I would choose for her: the column of brightly colored paper cranes spontaneously made and draped around a street sign close to Ground Zero; the tea setting covered in ash; a child sitting in a circle holding a lit candle, her gaze one of resolve and hope.

The photograph she chose was of the second plane slamming into the Twin Tower. I was horrified. What would her parents think? How would she live with this image? I calmly asked her why this particular picture.

"Because I don't want to forget," she said.

Peace is the act of remembering. War is the act of forgetting; otherwise, we would not repeat the horrors of human suffering over and over again.

Poetry is also an act of remembering, a gesture on behalf of what is possible. "[I]f you see the shadow of peace/make sure to touch it. . . ," writes Bryn Kass. The anthology you hold in your hands is a bow toward this kind of grace.

The poet Kenneth Rexroth writes, "The art of being civilized is the art of learning to read between the lies." Each of these award-winning poems written by children and adults inspired by the Nuclear Age Peace Foundation reads between the lies.

As I write this, we are a nation at war. President George W. Bush tells us in this fight against terrorism that "we will rid the world of evil," that "all options are on the table." The threat of nuclear war by our own hands, not to mention the tremors of unrest felt in Pakistan and India, places all humanity in a precarious position of risk and uncertainty. The phrase "dirty bomb" has entered our vocabulary with a dangerous passivity, like a film preview, "coming soon," what we can expect to see right before the featured action movie.

Peace requires actions of a different sort. The act of restraint. The act of listening. The act of compassion, to feel in one's body another point of view. Peace, like poetry, is an act of the imagination offering us a path toward our highest and deepest selves.

"The first disarmament is that between us," writes Bear Jack Gebhardt. Courage allows us to take those first brave steps toward a new way of being, a new way of seeing what we might become. For a community to embrace peace, we must first embrace each other.

These particular poets remind us through the power of words, images, and metaphors that our world is as delicate and strong as spider's silk. Indeed, we can create a tapestry of peace together in the name of all that holds us in love as human beings. We can begin to live differently.

> If peace were our greatest industry,
> harmony our best-selling product,
> and no one unemployed in its pursuit,
> this scene would be as common as chicory flowers in June
> as we soaked in solar pleasure and
> the simple beauty of humans in harmony
> at the jade green lake.
>
> —Claudia Lapp

May we read each one of these poems as a prayer. May we find inspiration in their courage to speak on behalf of peace. And may we be inspired to pick up our own pens and write our way home to a more sustainable world.

INTRODUCTION

# The Poetry of Peace
BY DAVID KRIEGER

W hen politicians speak of peace their words ring hollow, and one searches in vain these days for statesmen who rise above narrow nationalism. But when poets speak of peace, one senses deeper truths.

War has historically engendered a herd mentality. Peace, on the other hand, begins with the personal and moves outward. This gives poets a solid starting point for exploring the dimensions of peace.

Peace begins with the heart, an appropriate grounding for poets. Peace and poetry stand on common ground. Poet William Stafford describes this ground as "the field where the battle did not happen, where the unknown soldier did not die."

Our world, at once so beautiful and miraculous, yet so violent and in need of repair, cries out for peace. But where are the peacemakers? It is not easy to be a peacemaker in these times, but it is also not so difficult. It requires only vision and an act of will. Because it is not modeled by political leaders nor celebrated in the media, peace may seem distant. In fact, it is not so far away, not further than a personal decision to act for peace.

"Poetry," writes Pablo Neruda, "is an act of peace. Peace goes into the making of a poet as flour goes into the making of bread." It is also true that poetry, and certainly poetic acts, are key ingredients for creating peace. Both peace and poetry resonate with the language of the heart.

There is a famous photograph taken in America during the Vietnam War of a young woman placing a flower in the barrel of a soldier's rifle. The young woman stands before a rigid young soldier in his starched military outfit. She confronts his sternness and his rifle with her courage and a flower.

The two young people are standing face to face. The young man is armed with a weapon of death, standing unblinking, expressionless. The young woman is armed only with a flower. She speaks to the soldier symbolically in the language of the heart, her act a poem.

What is the young man to do when confronted by this gift? Perhaps he does not know. Perhaps he awaits orders. But how can the young woman's poetic act not have pierced his armor and opened his heart? How can one shoot a person who fights with flowers? To achieve the poetic moment when a flower trumps a rifle requires people who can see each other face to face, who can recognize the other's humanness. This is a feat not possible when a bomber pilot and his crew are flying at 30,000 feet above a peasant village or a city.

Brave young men and women also stood before the tanks in Tienanmen Square in Beijing. Courage and poetic acts know no boundaries. They are not the traits of any one people or culture, but traits that are found in ordinary people everywhere, ordinary people who are quite extraordinary.

Two—of many—heroes of the civil rights movement in the United States touched the core of poetry and the human spirit. A tired black seamstress, Rosa Parks, by her simple refusal to move to the back of the bus, said by her action that she, like all persons, deserved to be treated with respect and dignity. Martin Luther King's deep, resonant voice and profoundly poetic vision still sounds in our hearts. "I have a dream," he said and said again. He touched people everywhere with the vitality and validity of his poetic spirit. His dream was an invitation to others to dream and act for a more decent and humane world.

Bigotry and conformity are the enemies of both peace and poetry. They reinforce tendencies to inhumanity, greed and the concentration of power. They are qualities that undermine democratic societies and are antithetical to the poetic spirit.

The German poet and dramatist Bertolt Brecht wrote:

> General, man is very useful.
> He can fly and he can kill.
> But he has one defect:
> He can think.

Brecht identified the locus of vulnerability of any army. It must be composed of soldiers, who have the "defect" of being able to think. And yet, how often individual perspective is sacrificed on the altar of conformity. How often the sovereignty of conscience gives way to the conformity of militant and narrow nationalism.

What would happen if young people learned the language of poetry and peace in their schools? Would they be able to suspend their conscience to simply follow orders? Would they be able to turn their rifles on poor peasants or drop napalm bombs on peasant villages?

Tun Channareth, a Cambodian activist who lost both his legs to a landmine, prepared a poetic speech on behalf of the International Campaign to Ban Landmines when that organization won the Nobel Peace Prize in 1997. The speech was never delivered because the Nobel Committee would not provide translation from Channareth's native Khmer. In his speech, he states, "My handicaps are quite visible. They can remind us of the invisible handicaps we all have…the 'landmines of the heart.' These landmines inside can lead us to war, to jealousy, to cruel power over others. If we ban landmines of the heart along with landmines in the earth, the needs of the poor will take priority over the wants of the rich, the freedom of the dominated over the liberty of the powerful…. Together we can stop a coward's war that makes victims of us all."

His metaphor, "landmines of the heart," is powerful and poetic. He may have lost his legs to landmines, but he has not surrendered the peace and poetry in his heart. Despite his loss, he stands solidly committed to peace. How can one not embrace this man for his courage and for the poetry of his compassion?

Here is what he said about peace: "Peace is a path that is chosen consciously. It is not an aimless wandering but a step-by-step journey. It means compassion without concession, and peace without bowing to injustice. Loving kindness is the only way of peace." Tun Channareth is a peacemaker who speaks in poetry.

The great documents of our time include the language of poetry. The United Nations Charter begins: "We the Peoples of the United Nations determined to save succeeding generations from the scourge of war, which twice in our lifetime has brought untold sorrow to mankind…." In poetic words, it is a call to action, a call to peace, a call to end the "untold sorrow" of the world wars that the founders of the United Nations had experienced and that hovered ominously over their future.

The first article of the Universal Declaration of Human Rights also speaks in the language of poetry: "All human beings are born free and equal in dignity and rights. They are endowed with reason and conscience and should act towards one another in a spirit of brotherhood."

Does love of country mean one need love our world less or not at all?

Do people cease being people, deserving of respect and dignity, because they live on the other side of a line we call a border? There may be technical and legal differences in nationality and citizenship, but can borders create differences in the human spirit? Are not all people everywhere, as the Universal Declaration of Human Rights proclaims, "born free and equal in dignity and rights"?

I am a proponent of Earth Citizenship, a birthright of being born on our planet. This is an Earth Citizen Pledge that I wrote many years ago:

> I pledge allegiance to the Earth,
> and to its varied life forms;
> one world, indivisible,
> with liberty, justice and dignity
> for all.

And why not? Why not one world? Why not embrace the Earth and all its creatures?

The creative process is a mystery. How does a poet form words into a meaningful and moving whole? The poet Denise Levertov wrote this in a poem called *Making Peace*:

> But peace, like a poem,
> is not there ahead of itself,
> can't be imagined before it is made,
> can't be known except
> in the words of its making…

Peace may seem impossible, an impossible dream, but in the human spirit and our dreams there are no impossibilities. There will certainly be barriers, obstacles that must be overcome, as we move through uncharted territory, but not impossibilities. We have not the right to give up on peace or on each other.

Sadako Sasaki, a young girl dying from exposure to radiation following the bombing of Hiroshima, folded paper cranes in the hopes that her wishes for health and world peace would be realized. On one of the paper cranes she wrote this short poem: "I will write peace on your wings and you will fly all over the world."

And indeed Sadako's cranes have flown all over the world. Children everywhere know the story of Sadako and her courageous effort to survive. Today a statue of Sadako stands in Hiroshima Peace Memorial Park, and its base is always overflowing with brightly colored paper cranes brought and sent by children from Japan and throughout the world.

When Ukraine gave up its last nuclear weapons to Russia for dismantling in 1996, the defense ministers of the Ukraine and Russia and the US Secretary of Defense held a highly unusual ceremony. They gathered at a former missile base in the Ukraine where nuclear-armed missiles had once been aimed at the United States, and they planted sunflowers. The then US Secretary of Defense, William Perry, stated on the occasion: "Sunflowers instead of missiles in the soil will ensure peace for future generations." The planting of sunflowers where missiles had been was an unmistakable act of peace.

Peace and poetry meet and interact in mysterious and surprising ways. A poem can touch our hearts and inspire us to action. A poetic act can touch us, sometimes in even deeper ways, and compel us along the path to peace. A young woman places a flower in the barrel of a soldier's rifle, a young Chinese man stands in front of a tank before the eyes of the world, a tired black seamstress refuses to give up her seat to move to the back of the bus, a great civil rights leader shares his dream, a Cambodian landmine victim speaks of "landmines of the heart," a young Japanese girl folds paper cranes, and a Secretary of Defense plants sunflowers. All of these acts share a poetic spirit of peace that crosses all borders and reaches deep into our shared human spirit.

The poems in this book examine peace from many perspectives. They are filled with the wonder and magic of everyday life. They also express the sorrow and loss that war and violence bring. They speak to the fear and frustration that one may not be able to do enough to assure peace. They find peace rooted in relationships to each other, to other living things and to the earth. In these poems one finds a burning desire to do more to heal wounded spirits and our wounded earth. These poems combine the mystery of creativity with a longing for peace.

# The Poems

BY DAVID KRIEGER

The poems in this anthology are primarily the prize-winning poems in the Nuclear Age Peace Foundation's annual Barbara Mandigo Kelly Peace Poetry Awards, a contest initiated in 1996 "to encourage poets to explore and illuminate positive visions of peace and the human spirit." This book contains the prize-winning poems from the first seven years of the contest in three categories: adult, youth ages 13 to18, and children 12 years of age and under. Also included in this volume are poems by judges of the contest.

In sponsoring this contest among young people, the Foundation seeks to address an unfulfilled need, since, unfortunately, a poetic vision of peace is not emphasized, often not even acknowledged, in our classrooms. The contest itself is a form of peace education for youth and for adults as well.

Each year a committee of talented poets meets to select the winning poems. The chair of the committee, Perie Longo, states: "The writing of a poem is itself something like an act of peace in how it orders the storm of thought and passion until it settles on the page, so we were pleased to see so many poets of all ages address this exciting and necessary subject. The process of discovering the winning poems was one of reading and re-reading until certain poems surfaced, the committee first looking for original content, and then refinements of craft and music. We looked for poems with a clear, distinct voice that could turn the abstraction of peace into a definite experience we could take in and feel, and lastly to have the poem shine off the page."

The poetry awards honor the memory of Barbara Mandigo Kelly, an extraordinary woman of quiet and firm determination to build a better world by poetic words and deeds. One of her poems is included in this collection. She was the wife of one of the founders of the Nuclear Age Peace Foundation, who has provided an essay about her in this volume.

We hope that from these poems you will take courage and make your presence felt by your own words and creative acts of peace.

# THE POETRY
# OF PEACE

# EARTHSCAPES

David Ray

# *Flying Over Cheyenne Mountain*

*"The reflection that for the first time in history the phenomenon of a great city, like New York, being there in the morning and not being there in the afternoon could perfectly well occur."*

—James Gould Cozzens

You look down on the mountains snow-capped,
as lovely as when John Muir beheld them,

but you do not know which is hollowed out
for gnomes to enact their Wagnerian opera,

some cities gone to the boom of kettle drums,
others to oboes and firestorms, violins so vibrato

that earth will shake as ash overtakes distant suburbs
and men become writhing flesh, no better than

earthworms tormented. It is the hour we all fear
we will come to, when the maestro's fulfillment

will lie in conducting the final performance,
so explosive that the audience will be consumed

in the adoration. "So much talent!" We have said
for years as we paid scripters and set designers

and bit players happy to sing in the chorus.
Is this climax long planned not wished devoutly—

our first human feat to be seen from the stars?
Until they fall, all the mountains are holy save one.

PHYLLIS COBB

# *Minato-ku, Tokyo*

I walk the dogs
in morning
darkness
among embassies
and diplomatic
ghosts.

No trace
of previous
war.

No planes
droning overhead
on zulu time.

Raucous crows
instead,
meander above
the morning.

One brave
old tree
listens.

JOYCE CAINES

# *Streets of Tashkent*

Dry dust of chilla
doma walls pink in the late day sun.

A piece of corrugated sheet metal
lies crumpled on the street.

There is a man.

His undershirt is thirsty
for his bodywater and salt.

He stoops over long handle hammer
                                 levering nails.
One foot steadies the metal
the other is in the dust.

Infant son swaggers behind him

bent nails in the street
scattered under the shade of walnut tree.

Barefoot he dances naked
                                 near metal edge.

BEAR JACK GEBHARDT

# On Allard St.

In the night in the quiet after love
we are disarmed—at peace with each other.

Our moment there envelops the armed earth,
settling into silos where missiles wait,
fogging radar screens, muddling generals' minds
bringing drowsiness to soldiers on watch.

What we do in our private lives does count.
Who we are, what we love, how we make peace
one by one, two by two, three by three...ahh,
the peace of the world is built in this way.

Your openness to me—trusting, eager,
vulnerable—makes our lusty union whole.
Missiles are rusted by our moist love words.
Your giggles jam the guns of combatants.
This softness between us in our day life
melts the metal helmets the soldiers wear.

Our relationship infiltrates war rooms.
Our balanced love helps make the decision
against mobilization. Last night's love—
no need today for retaliation.

We begin here: first each with our own peace,
then together, one and one making two,
and from here, then, the world must bend to us
as surely as dawn bends to the night, lifts
her veil to reveal the light, new day...

The first disarmament is that between us.
From here, from this room on Allard Street,
                              the world is set at peace.

ANTHONY RUSSELL

# *After Vespers at the Monastery, Abiquiu, NM*

All is in shadow here, but light
still pours down Gallinas Cañon
from the West, firing
the yellow tips of cottonwood
and oak by the Chama River.
In moments they too are dark,
leaving only the East wall
of the towering mesa enflamed.
Silence tumbles from a fading sky.
In an hour the moon will rise
with its lesson in patience.
My narrow bed waits.

CLAUDIA LAPP

# *Lake*

It can be this good,
life on our green planet:
give us a lake of silken waters, spring-fed.
Drop in people of all fleshy shapes, colors and ages,
speaking many languages, side by side.
Let the water be various shades of jade green
with tiny fishes to edge between toes.
Let the orange lifeguard's banner float on the clean breeze,
Let each cloud caravan move across perfect sky,
each leaf respond to each strand of summer breeze,
each ant and dandelion dance its part in harmony.
And if there be disharmony,
let it be forgotten, here and now,
by Irish and Anglo, Arab and Jew, Black and White.
Let the AK automatics of hate drop from bruised shoulders.
If there be heartache, let the winds carry it away, here and now, and
if it remain, let it find its source and be healed.
If there be weariness of old age, let the waters smooth it.
Let the waters smooth us all to rounded green pebbles,
serene.

If peace were our greatest industry,
harmony our best-selling product,
and no one unemployed in its pursuit,
this scene would be as common as chicory flowers in June
as we soaked in solar pleasure and
the simple beauty of humans in harmony
at the jade green lake.

AMY RIDER

# *Nagasaki Trees*

I.

How could one
Be glum
Looking at trees?
Though their leafy arrows
may point, green, to the ground.

There is something tranquil in chlorophyll.
It is a drug.
It ought to be banned
In un-peaceful land.

II.

Through the heat of melted sidewalks,
And babies squealing like eagles,
Still green fire
Reaches up to Heaven.
Ever reaching,
Never losing faith
In the blue linen.

And for that reason
Their faith preserves them
Like honey over mushrooms,
Hundreds of years
Till they die
And reach their sky.

ALEC STEURY

# *Chinese Moon*

A sad star
over a crimson
Bangkok sea
slowly settling down to sleep,
a softly dropping flare
cross the eastern sky.

Seven suns and
seven moons.

Along the shore
footsteps in the sand
wash away with night,
disappear.

Sleep beautiful child,
sleep.

GREGORY COLEMAN

# *Circles, ever widening*

The path to Swayambunath
cuts across rice paddies. The dikes newly
cut; the earth sheened by the shovel.
When the rains come, the field's mirrored clouds
float, disappear into one dike, emerge, cross the watery earth.

Across these waters, I hear thunder.
The army men are playing with rifles, shooting
at a roadside earthen breastwork—head-high, just
enough so that a tall man walking needs to stoop.

I prefer this path. Not the yellow flagged road
where I wonder if I am too tall, the dike too weak,
a bullet named for me.

A Vietnam adolescence: reading Gandhi and King,
Black Elk, finding out why I will not.

I am circumnavigating
the earth by foot and thumb, boat, bus.
At twenty-six, I still refuse to
practice death, to see the outlined man
as enemy, as other.

I watch the women fold their shawls,
hitch up their saris and take
pale green, clumped rice seedlings, line
up, take a single stalk, plant their feet
unseen, clutch the earth, and plunge seedling
and arm through the blue sky into
the unseen earth.

Only later when I am on
the paddy paths, the sun
floating in their watery skies
mottled blue and white
when the guns thunder

I stop, put down my parcels of rice, tea,
potatoes wrapped with folded newspaper
and thin, dark string, sit.

Alone, an idle bee lights, grows silent beside me.
I roll between the skies, see my face
hover in the clouds that break
into concentric circles
ever widening.

GLENNA LUSCHEI

# *Peace in the Forest*

You become a dweller of the forest, Asians say,
after you have ceased your labors and disposed
of your shrine, even your iron kettle and saki jug.

You leave behind your yukata and obi.
Spiders will spin your clothes,
beetles caught in webs crust your jewels.

Sheds in the clearing may offer shelter.
Here, too, we live in goosepens of the redwoods
listening for the industry of nurse trees

who raise new generations from their bark.
Here, we relinquish the crown, no more to hear
corona from the high tension wires.

We turn our swords into plowshares,
our plowshares into harps.
We dwell in forest now, our only office

to hang our harps upon the trees. Willows become
our instruments. The cedars voice our lamentations.

KRISTIN TRAICOFF

# *Clouds*

And now the day is over and
the clouds melt into my mosque ceilinged sky.
They seem to shroud the sunset,
shroud the winking stars,
shroud the infinite shadows of the pines
calling too much attention
to themselves.
    (but you know that
        in their divinity they create the entrance to the sun
    you know that
        all that is noble and all that is simple converge within them
    you know that
        tears of poets condense to form their liquid
    you know that
        they are peace—flowing flying freely
        unaware of their depth
        simply existing in the cool of the night and day
        hovering above the earth like the breath of seraphim
        and finally slipping onto our skin in ancient and honest drops
        which do not seize but drip softly around the soul)
Welcome to the universe,
Kindly step off the earth into the clouds.

EVANNE WILSON

# *Sunflower*

A beautiful bright
lion's mane blowing
in the wind shaking
his head, it is whispering
to all the creatures. A
pansy, a parrot squawking
in a forever tune, a rose blood spilling from
another one's prey. A gardenia, a white
tiger roar to the beat of
the wind. Graceful poppies,
the antelope running
in the whispering grass
but the sunflower, the lion
standing tall and proud
above them all, clearly
the ruler of all flowers.

GAVIN SCHNEIDER

# *Sacred Dust*

The harsh summer struggle
     between the yellow morning.

Night rains; dirt and soil and death.

The rain from the ground was like the forest.

I planted the shadow with my bare hands.

Peace rains light and happiness.

Quiet wind drifts across the mellow trees.

After the approach to the mountains,
     the bouquet of silence
         greeted me beneath the night.

The sacred dust above the trees
     settled upon the Earth.

SOJOURNER KINCAID ROLLE

# *Where the Hum Begins*

I am in a place
where water rolls across the stones
rippling in ranges
too high for human tones to mimic.

It is a place
where mountains loom over land
so low it is almost level with the sea.

In the distance,
I can hear
water falling fast
from a high plateau;
   brushing the slope of the solid earth
at sharp angles, diving
into the flow;
where it falls, a continuous splash issues.

It is at this place I dwell —
   between calm and turmoil
between yang and yin
   between memory and amnesia
between today and tomorrow
   between sate and want.

In the magic hour —
   when the tide changes.
In the right moment —
   where each second becomes the next.
In the pull of the moon
   while the water ebbs and flows.

In this place, I stand on land
    rocky like a river;
land where boulders abide
    deep within the soil.

It is a place of peace
    even as on the billowing sea.

JEFFREY HARTMAN

# Ode to the Swans

As two swans glide gently over
the moon lit lake
they lift off into the air
like a silent wind gliding over the tops
of the trees. As they land
not a ripple heads
to the cold shore.
They are like two white angels.
I wish I could fly like them,
their necks come out like a shooting arrow
to pierce the cold sky
but so gentle how snow falls to the
ground.

SETH BOWMAN

# The Peaceful City

The peaceful city was by a river,

The river was by the ocean,

The city had a church,

The church was very peaceful,

There was a cemetery,

The cemetery was quiet,

It was so quiet it would scare you,

The ocean had a salty smell,

The best part of the city was

the sound of the stream moving

so swiftly.

# MEMORIES

J. KEIKO LANE

# *Winter Tomatoes*

I. Of Manzanar 1942

"We didn't know where they had taken him. Right at harvest
time. Tomatoes. Winter crop. Told us to pack. Only what we
could carry. But the harvest almost ready and our father, they
took him. No one thought they would take us. Honor roll, I
was. High School. Until the harvest. White teachers told us no
way they'd take us. Honor roll. No worry. This place, cold in
winter, too cold to grow. Lots of ice, wind, snow. Jack rabbits.
That's it. Finally our father returned. Want to know what
happened to tomato crop. Took us before harvest. They
probably kept. Father taken to Tule Lake, where they took
spies. Thought he was a traitor, selling secrets over seas,
sending weapons with the harvest."


II. Los Angeles 1996

In her spine folded shuffle,
my Grandmother points out
weeds in the thick green
tomato beds. Slowly she can reach
some of the fruit, garden

built at waist height by her sons.
On cushions she sits in the sun
a stray rabbit adopts her,
sits by her feet eating the green leaves
she feeds it, watching her tomatoes.

BARBARA MANDIGO KELLY

# *For the Year of Peril, 1942*

Now in destruction grows a hardy seed,
Impervious to rubbling bombs' assault,
Unspoiled by cannons' calculating greed
And unconfined in fear's concealing vault.
Nursed in a soil more native than the earth,
Older than chaos which disturbs our land,
Scorned and denied, forgotten from its birth
By all the universe, from the blood-fed sand
It springs again and makes a mighty tree
Angry and proud and reaching through the sky.
Here bursts the beauty of eternity
In flowered symbols—though our tortured cry
Should shake its terrible and tender roots,
It yet shall succor us with ripened fruits.

DAVID KRIEGER

# Dance of Hiroshima

I watched you dance
the dance of Hiroshima,
your eyes filled with
a sorrow so deep
it opened your heart
and small birds flew away.

With faltering steps
you became a child,
a maiden, a mother,
a widow, a mourner.
You stumbled and fell,
you picked yourself up,
grew wings and flew away.

I watched you dance
your fear and anger
your youth and magic.
I watched you rise
from the ashes, fly
with the wings of a crane
and float back to Earth.

## *atomic garden*

dressed in paper white and pink
restless schoolchildren and old cherry trees
surround us in the peace park

tiny ears and eyes open like blossoms
bending to the tender voice of the guide
stones rattle in our hearts

among themselves brown sparrows
quarrel for scattered seeds a baby
rabbit trembles

as we tremble now for you laid
belly-down in a hollow under the bald
moon

face boiled empty and pocketed scars
Hiroshima
stopped like a watch

through ashes a grandmother
carried her burden
a *furushiki* of bones

she brought her daughter back
wrapped like a gift
some parents found only buttons

all night the children swim
searching for innocence
under the lid of a dreamless lake

SYLVIA CRAFTON

# *the peacemaker*

they say he got worse as he got older
and no one who ever saw him bawl and swear
or raise his clinched fist into the air
as though to lift his profanities heaven high
ever cared to dispute it
he was mad they said and he was
in his head and his spirit
it was the first few days after
he got the letter that were the worst
they could hear him screaming and bawling
and his little mixed breed dog
with the cornucopia ears constantly yapping
and all manner of knocks and bangs
coming from his garage
the ones brave enough to go and see
found him at his workshop table
hands bleeding veins in his forehead bulging
tears streaming down his face
the little dog still yapping
see this letter the damned senator sent me
he waved it in front of them
he said friendly fire killed my boy
ain't no fire friendly when it kills your own
and he went back to his banging and pounding
as though he'd never heard of a forge
sparks would fly but the metal wouldn't bend
they told him he was crazy
war makes a man crazy he shouted
and i'm gonna beat this sword into
a ploughshare if it kills me yet
i'm gonna do it in honor of my boy

KAREN KOVACIK

# Requiem for the Buddhas of Bamiyan

*"If we gain something, it was there from the beginning.*
*If we lose something, it is hidden nearby."*

—Ryokan

Between the empire of China
   and the empire of Rome,
in an oasis along the Silk Road,

you heard pomegranates change hands
   in Latin and Farsi and Greek.
Chinese generals, Persian merchants,

inventors of gunpowder and algebra,
   fanciers of rhubarb and bronze:
all conducted their commerce

in your shadow: you
   who saw monasteries cut from mountains,
you who were sculpted out of sandstone,

who listened to the whispers of Christians;
   who welcomed Muslims and Manicheans,
disciples of Nestor and Zoroaster.

Leopards and lions rolled past you
   in their cages, actors
mimicked peacocks and parrots, travelers

who'd thirsted through the Taklamakan Desert
        gave thanks to plural gods.
You who survived Genghis Khan's cannon,

who saw the British retreat, then Soviets and Americans,
        you whom the Taliban ringed
with burning tires blacking your face,

you with dynamite in your groin, you witness
        to starving farmers, to secret schools for girls:
for fourteen centuries you stood fast

still as Siddhartha
        on the night of his enlightenment,
as much a part of this valley as the wind.

Who will know you now by your absence,
        remembering your before?
When the night comes, who will know you?

When the ash falls, who will know you?
        After earthquakes and eclipses,
wherever there is fire,

how to feel you filling us and leaving us,
        abiding in the grottoes
of our breath?

MARINA WILSON

# *Poem for MJ Polo*

what I mean to tell you
started in Saigon          in Ho Chi Minh City
outside the war memorial
a man, missing a foot asked me—*what country miss*
he wanted to sell me postcards, but I had no words

nothing to say     *my country packs metal in      its veins*
*the gun under the pillow      has a barrel at each end*

I grew up on re-runs
Watched M*A*S*H on television, but that was Korea
Gary Tufts wore drag to get out of Vietnam
     they sent him anyway
then there's my uncle who doesn't talk about that year
like a deep hole he walks around

and the man, he asked me again
*what country—*
and the answer lodged itself in my throat

I know this is an old story—

children on dirt roads, a man holding another man's head in the air,
fire and more fire, the medal an American soldier sent back
to Vietnam, an apology

Irma kept chattering     I wanted her to go away
I wanted everyone to go away—the man, his one leg

later, we were talking about war
and MJ the Canadian was saying something
about *but isn't life cheaper here*
the line about poor people not loving as much
and I had to look away from him and toward the sky behind us
because the words pulled away from me

this is what I wanted to say

on the train to Hanoi, I watched a father and his son

a delicate, wide-faced boy, with an open gaze
he kept staring at me and saying something
to his father      his father smiling, said something back
and tried to put the boy to sleep
he swept his palm across the boy's back and ran his fingers through his hair
the boy kept standing up in the berth to look at everyone on the train
then his father would coax him back and try again to put the boy to sleep
this went on for over an hour
the man holding the boy, stroking him
singing quietly

SUSAN LLOYD McGARRY

# *Washing*

Walking towards the clothesline,
careful in the night, I measure
my steps as if on a tightrope.

A dark shape
becomes familiar in my arms—
the flannel nightgown cool to my touch.

Each piece of clothing smells of the outside,
fresh.  Morning in my arms,
though the lines above me melt into night.

The wooden clothespins shut
in my hand before I drop them in the bucket,
as my mother dropped them, and her mother and hers...

I stand in the mystifying dark
and listen
to a lonesome peeper.

Could we wash words? Claim them
back from buying and selling,
from the lack of care? Wash them one

by one, hang them to dry,
then gather them in our arms,
the ordinary words.

Would you do this?
Would you use them to say
what you mean?

To say *love*,
to say *new*, to say
*now?*

DEBBIE PARVIN

# *Peacemaker*

She never lit a candle in a vigil.
She never raised a voice for human rights.
She slept on public benches in the summer—
In basement shelters on cold, winter nights.

She never held a sign and demonstrated.
She moved no one to action with her words,
But in the park each day, by roaring traffic,
She knelt to share her bread crumbs with the birds.

SUSAN MILES GULBRANSEN

# *The Intruders*

A coyote's howl carries through the night air
circles the hills and mountains
breaks into the darkened womb of my bed and covers
        the room has no corners, no colors
        invisible in early morning dark
        sounds muffled
until the primeval wail charges the night
again and again
followed by a shriek and another howl.
Then the yipping takes over, short, staccato cries
        tonight they are meant to rattle the prey
        hunt down the frightened, the doomed
more join the rabble
the chase is on
the yelps build into a crescendo, a frenetic rhythm
        faster  louder  higher-pitched
then a sudden scream rises above all
the yipping slows, stops.
Is the hunt over? Was there an escape?
Or has the meal begun?

I try for sleep,
but an ancient memory awakes.

RAMONA BACA-HODROFF

# *That Day*

Home on a chill autumn day, laying on my bed,
muscles relaxing (and feeling)
the cartilage disks of my back
d    e    c    o    m    p    r    e    s    s    i    n    g,
the final twitches of my digits
as the last of the day's tension exits, flowing out of my
                                        finger tips,
my kitten, barely audibly, landing next to me and purring like the
                            smooth running engine of a new Mustang,
rubbing her damp nose on my cheek
as she suckles my ear lobe,
searching for milk,
my favorite singer's voice
lazily flowing through my head,
a lullaby...
I drift towards oblivion...

Waking up to
my best friend's head on my chest,
hearing the deep breathing from her smoker's lungs,
the faint smell of her
latest favorite perfume
filling my nose, her arm across my torso,
her body's very close to mine
(she's as warm as my teddy bear was when I was six years old)—
just being close,
just being friends,
just loving the chemistry we've shared...

My kitten is still purring, now wildly and with abandon...

Right now I am happy. I want this moment frozen, perfectly,
                                          in my mind.

# *September 11*

i saw a city on the morning news
where it rained glass like bright butterflies

i saw a man on the television
determined to destroy for his truth

i saw a woman in the evening paper
clasping the red white and blue against her grief

i saw the people with upturned faces
looking toward the heart of the sky

i saw that day a fragile heaven
but stronger than our fears

# DREAMS
## AND FEARS

DAVID CHORLTON

# *Nuclear Lullaby*

Go to sleep children, and don't worry
anymore for the people who saw
the flash so bright it changed the world.
Don't think about them running
with fire standing up like hairs
along their spines.  Think of the trees
growing back in Hiroshima's ashes.

Sleep well and don't worry
about the plant burning down.
It only happens at Chernobyl.
Not to you.  Your sheets
are white and clean.  Leave the lamp on
all night if you want to.

Never read in bed.  Close your eyes
and drink your milk.  Rest assured
that it is pure.  If a bad dream
should awaken you, think of the cows.
The cows are happy.
Cows always are. Even those

who raised their heads a moment
when the bomb lit up the sky,
then lowered them and went on chewing.

VIVIAN C. SHIPLEY

# Digging Up Peonies

Overcoming fear of stalks that are too close,
I remind myself it's a Lexington, that mist

on fields meant rattlesnakes curled in rows
of corn would be cold, sluggish. Like prying

out potatoes with my fingers, I dig up tubers
as if I could lift my father, seeded with cancer,

if only for a day from gravity, from ground.
My parents know what I know — this is the end;

they will not return to this house my father built.
No refugee in Kosovo, wheelbarrowing

his grandmother to safety, I will bring as much
of Kentucky, of their dirt as I can carry with me

on our flight to Connecticut. A bride, moving
to New Haven over thirty years ago, I have

not taken root. I cannot explain this urge
to go to creekstone fences my father stacked,

dig up box after box of peonies I will bank
into granite piled along my side garden

so my father can see pink, fuchsia blossoming
from his bed. Is this what revision is, change

of location, spreading, to retell my story
another time, in another soil? Unable to untie

what binds me to Kentucky, to bones of all
those who are in my bones, I will save what

I can of my mother, of my father from this earth,
from the dissolution that binds us after all.

KEITH ANTAR MASON

# lovers on ground zero

we drugged ourselves through human history to glow in the dark in the shadow box of this nation's terror we blew up on shore and sit on the front porches getting our heads dredded we still die poor hunger gripping our stomachs when the launch would occur we would have never have had a say about the pushed button the choice would have been made at 1600 and we would be wondering if the trash was gonna get picked up if mama would get off crack cause another baby was on the way or would we have swept clean the brown dirt in front of our houses down near the delta our skin darkened from our days in the sun eating a slice of watermelon listening to the tinny radio making the announcement the greens would have been good—good for a last meal we would go out back and look at the sky one last time there would be nowhere we could hide again from the night riders streaking against the wind's belly now in the sky we would have swallowed peace—blinked like the banger in the drive-by not wanting to kill anybody who then goes home wondering if it was his gun that killed that little girl playing in the yard mcdonalds would still have made a profit over burger king the rush for lunch and to get back to the office would have been an ironic twist on the west coast that second mocha for the extra push would not be needed and maybe being one of those unemployable brothers who would have given up on ever finding a job would be one of the most blessed cause while he was slipping off his clothes and laying in bed next to her in the late afternoon they would burn to death from being on ground zero lovers and maybe the color of their skin would not matter if as they fell back down like ash like that man who remembered after they cremated the man in the glass booth how small was the amount of his ashes that were left that much evil that little amount of ashes but at last there would be peace on this planet now a dirty snow ball with a strange orbit this is not what i want to dream about in my sleep this is not the excuse why black gangs seem so anxious for extinction this is not what i want

peaceout to mean when i say it to end a phone conversation i am
mindful these days of how i speak of peace as a black man
and why i want it to fill the streets and the homes where i live i want
jazz music to be the only explosion of my thoughts acted upon my
optic nerve intact my vision of deserts and rocks so red that you want
to lay naked in the earth's arms and hum for me to want this may
seem strange for me to know that i like the heat of deserts on my bare
feet listening to the earth seeing the green river flow a field of gerbera
daisies in full bloom and swimming naked in the gulf of mexico to
hear drowned slaves speak their names i want a clear peace a peace on
purpose with no threat and don't i have a say in this matter this new
moon

GARY J. WHITEHEAD

# *Arboretum*

Then you will have held something beautiful —
the hand of the old one dying by degrees,
the bloom of the almost undone season —
and you will have seen that, even now,
the scars — dark rivers, overgrown cities
of light — might heal still in the way
the aging and the broken have sometimes
of rising suddenly despite whatever sores
or the atrophy of the body might bear
upon a soul — and maybe you'll see it
in some place so ordinary as a public garden
and its most private space, late one afternoon,
leaning against a fence, taking the last
bright bell of morning glory like your great-
grandmother's open hand, and you'll hold it
as if it's the last bloom left on earth,
and you'll hold it as if to empty into it
the ringing in your ears that evens out
suddenly to birdsong and the buzz of bees
there in the garden's remotest place,
late one summer, late in the millennia,
safe with the company you keep, safe as the earth,
and the blue, silent bell closing into sleep.

Rebecca Durkin

# A Night to Travel

I can recognize the sound
of hopes defeated (I recall it from
the thumping of my own) and
today I went deaf from the cacophony.
seems the world has gone awry,
and all I seek is that soft melody
to sing me sweetly through the night.

Certainly I can take the road —
find the nightingale that Keats
told me would rest my worried head;
I can trouble her for a lullaby
and hope she'd romaticize my living.
But I'm in no shape for such a trek —
I'm a hopeless wreck in need of
A quick fix.  Take to the road I will!

But it is not nature I shall seek.
merely the g-g-g-grove of the
tires over the rain-slicked streets,
and the clickclickdiggaclick
of the car signals — the sweet
melodies of escape, of life on
the run with no time for the beauty.
Because life itself is all I can
handle this night.  Life and the way it wails.

Emily Vizzo

# Untitled

I have traversed the earth
through the heat of a deep dark silence
in pursuit of a cool green
and old brick walkways.

I have watched paintings
through the glare of windowpanes
in pursuit of a certain knowledge
standing in the paint.

In pursuit of God
I have dabbed out doubts
and knelt in the dim
raising prayers to saints.

I have met a mouth in the dark
through a curtain of shame
in pursuit of companionship
and the feel of arms around me.

In pursuit of magic
I have baited fairy-traps
and tossed pennies into spilling fountains
naming wishes as I stood.

I pursued until my legs fell away
and now I swim content
through legions of peace
and let life come to me.

Carefully I crafted a loop with the string
and tossed it into the river.

I never caught a fish with buttercups
or a knotted string.

But I saw them swimming by
in fleets of flashing silver

And for me, that was
enough.

MARINA MOSES

## *Theseus Slaying the Minotaur,*
## *a  Sculpture by Antoine-Louise Barye*

Oh, is that how it happened?
Theseus, upright and strong
held the monstrous Minotaur at arm's length
and slew him with one stroke.
But this Minotaur is not dead yet.
See how he grapples with Theseus
pulling at his iron body
— only mortal after all —
how easily his legs would buckle
his knife point away from the trusting
blank cow eye.
How easily history could change —
Man not triumph,
not take the world for his own.
Theseus, drop the knife, let this fallen half-demon be.
Let him cry on your shoulder.
Let us be.

KRISTEN BISHOP

# *Dreaming Peace*

Whenever I dream, I dream Peace.
Somehow it just comes naturally to me.
Sometimes I dream about my horse
running freely through the pale white flowers in a meadow.
I can tell when someone is dreaming peace
because they have a large sparkle in their eye.
But when people dream about war
their eyes are red with fury.
When I dream peace I see a feather,
light as a grain of sand,
and soft as silk.
I know peace, yet not many people do.

SASHA G. HAMDANI

# I Want to Touch the World

I want to be as free as a wild horse
trampling through the forest brush. I want to
grow as graceful as a fawn, fur as soft as its
eyes. I want to sing like the whale sings on its
midnight escapade. I want to be as mystifying
as a glassy pond hidden deep in the forest. I
want to be as beautiful as a young cardinal
learning to fly. I want to be colored a
heartwarming pink, like an ever-blooming rose
outside a frosted window. I want to be the
breeze between the trees, and the water after
a pulsing comes. I want to be stars falling
through the sky, jumping through the clouds,
and waiting for the sunlight to dim. I want to
be as cunning as a fox. I want to be the eyes of
a tiger burning through the grass, camouflaged
until it feels captivity. I can help you. I can
help you like I help the sun go to sleep, and the
moon arise, and the nature be born. I want to
reach out and touch the world with delicate
fingers, releasing the peace through my
fingertips. I want to bind the wound between
love and hate.

CARA RUBINSTEIN

# *The Peace of the Night*

As the night's moon gives his light
children feel the warmth of peace
as their dreams go on in their heads
of the howling wolf
cuddling them in her fur.
As the stars float down on their cheeks.

The wind blows through
the daisy's petals.
As the fairies in the roses
wish for people to solve their problems
in a peaceful way.

War is like an ugly face
laughing and making fun of you
as you stand lost in the cold and all
you hear are woodpeckers pecking
the trees.

The magic of the night's peace
comes when everyone is sleeping
Don't you wish it came out more often?

MARINA MOSES

# *This Is My Fear*

This is my fear today:
that they will cut down all the trees.
That's the one thing I hate about spring
They trim the tops of the trees
and every year I am afraid
that they will go too far
and all the new green
will turn brown
and die.

This is my fear today:
that they will think me insensitive
for while I worry that my trees will be cut down
over there they are cutting people
with machine guns and chain saws
and the land is turning dead, and brown
and all the new people
and all the old people
fall
and die.

This is my fear today:
that they will go too far.

That we will go too far.

JONATHAN NAGATA

# *Forced from Home*

Dear Mother,
I smell the smoke of the burning buildings.
I feel the fire, burning in my heart.
The hum of the bombers is stuck in my mind.
The cries of the children fuel my fear.
Ashes fly up and blind me.
All of the men, filled with sorrow.
All of the women, shedding their tears.
Will I ever see you again?

CHRYSS YOST

# *Graduation Day*

In the middle of the ceremony, it hits:
how vulnerable we are, and always were,
bright American fish inside a barrel.

The Mylar balloons and bouquets
are suddenly a beacon
for every sociopathic sniper
in the state.

   An epiphany,
to think I wasn't watching, and now
the news sinks in:
how suddenly it all
gets blown apart, in Columbine
or Palestine or New York City.
The world at war, if not here,
   not this morning.
One good blow and even a sturdy
house collapses into cards.

The stadium of faces is too bare,
too innocent. Who wouldn't see
how much we stood for.
   There's too much security
and not enough to stop the bullet
I imagine being sent from A to B.

A rabbit thinking like a raptor,
I hate how easily I see it, how I
   become the terrorist
selecting a position in the crowd.

I'm tired of being careful.
I need peace to be more than a strong fence;
not just the sandy strip of beach that holds
the sharks inside the oceans;
a better dog, not just a thicker leash.

GENE KNUDSEN HOFFMAN

# *I Am Waiting*

I am waiting
for yesterday to turn
          purple—flashing
as I see it fresh with today's
          new sight.
And I am waiting
for history to read
          like love
because the words are
trembled with compassion.
And I am waiting
          for the song
to swell from a million,
million throats
because we've learned
how
     to
          save
               one
                    another.

ROSELYN CREWSE

# *The Sound of Peace*

Peace comes without a warning quietly
As a whisper, softly as a kiss
Brushed against a cheek

War announces itself at the top of its lungs
Breathing fire, how can Mankind survive the need

For power and land without brandishing weapons or
Threats of nuclear war?

Such power frightens everyone except
The foolish and the greedy

Someone will always play the game
Without rules, without conscience, without regard
To the consequences

We must each try to find peace at least
Within ourselves, pray that evil will not triumph, while
Time and sanity brings a quiet peace

On tiptoe so as not to disturb the
Sleeping beast we weave our way around the
Specter of war, the devil's feast

There we may find hidden from view
The treasure we call peace

BRIAN STEMPECK

## *a moment of faith*

a dragonfly floated alone
in the center of a pool
dancing lifelessly among
ripple shadows.
it gently collided with the rope
that divides shallow end from deep
and tried to pull itself from the water

wings are too heavy.

In the deep end, an autistic boy named David lay down on the end of
the diving board. On any other day, the children behind him would
have screamed their impatience, and he would have stood dumbly until
his mother pried him away. He had not touched the water all summer.

It was the first day of fall, the pool was empty, and David gazed
at the turquoise below in silence. After what must have seemed like hours
in a world where his impulses were rational, his mumbling coherent,
David rose with a strange smile on his face, sighed the sigh of angels and
went
    limp
          unto
               the
                    water.

Three waves expanded from a ring around the boy,
faded to the shallow end,
and consecutively drove the dragonfly on top of the rope,
high above the water's reach.
David swam to his father's arms,
the dragonfly sputtered its wings and flew away,
and for a second
I believed.

WILL NUNZIATA

# *Gramma*

She
> not to be confused with withering
>> She
>>> not to be confused with
>>> the pyramids

She a cook
> She a warrior
>> She a mind

She
> not to be confused with ache and pain
>> She in white
>>> She in sweaters

She with pride
> She with thought
>> She with song

She
> not to be confused with crackles or creaks
>> or falls
> She with light
>> She with sight
>>> She a reflection

She
> not to be confused with earrings or dictionaries or wood floors
> She a summer
>> She a voice
>>> She a shine

She
> not to be confused with confusion or lamentation or frowns.
> She a mitten
>> She an unlocked diary
>>> She a door of a castle

She

        not to be confused with a puddle

        She an ocean

               She a seagull

                      She an angel with flight

She

        not to be confused with sleep

               She not ready

                   She with life

                        **She forever**

HEATHER TURNER

## *Peace Defined*

Peace is...
    a Christmas stocking

a heart shaped Valentine
    fishing on a quiet lake

hunting four leaf clovers
    a red rose

           walking a dog

a sunset
    planting a tree

    LADYBUGS!
sheets airing on a clothesline

    construction paper
bread rising

    the sweet smell after a summer rain
a jack-o-lantern

    stamp collecting
birthday cake with lots of frosting

           eating POPcorn

sleeping in

Peace is not a destination we reach
  but rather
              the brief moments
    of JOY
  we discover along the way.

KETT MURPHY

# What is Peace

One day I met peace for the first time
and I asked her what she was
and she said to me,
"Peace is both sight and sound
and feeling and idea
Peace is happiness and joy
but tranquility and calm at the same time
Peace is what you feel after you do something that you know is right
and peace is lying on your back in sweet grass looking up at
big white clouds that roll by
in a picture perfect blue sky
Peace is when nothing seems to go wrong for you
and all you can do is smile"
Peace said this to me and then
she told me to tell everyone I knew
so I'm telling you

KRISTEN VON HOFFMANN

# *Happy*

My feet—wheels bumple over the gravel as Jack
                    pulls the leash
        then me and Jack
we glide
onto smoothness that wraps around the vast bean of grass
        When I look onto the park
my eyes feel happy, looking at the openness...
As we skate by the stream I hear an empty thumping like a
hollow
plastic bottle
lapping the
wall.
I look and it's a boy bumping his
drum for the
geese. I love this time at dusk when my long day is calmed
by
        cold.

# *signs of peace?*

he
told    me    to
write    a    poem
in the    shape    of a
peace    sign.    i said
he was    crazy.    i'm good,
but i'm    not    that good.
but, heck,    it    can't hurt
to try.    mama    always
said i    could    do what-
ever    i wanted. i    just
wish    i    had    a    clue
as    to    what    that    could
be.    Y'know,    maybe
i'll be a mango today.

Marlee J. Gluck

# *Peace*

Peace is when you get along
with other people
Peace is when people encourage
each other when they're not good
at something.

Peace is like happiness shooting up
from the earth's crust.
Peace can do magic when
people feel her love for each other
in their heart.

Peace can never be broken
not even if the whole world
drops on top of her.
Peace is my friend.

BRYN KASS

# *What is Peace*

Is it a cat or a dog
or a person we will never know
but whoever can touch the shadow of peace
will live in harmony.
If peace could jump through legs
or breathe into minds
maybe everything bad could stop.
Maybe peace could bring alive
what's been dead.
So if you see the shadow of peace
make sure to touch it.
If peace makes a home run
give her a high five!
But if all of these things
are not true, well we will never know,
but just remember if you see the shadow of peace
make sure to touch it
and all of a sudden if everything is well again
you'll know that peace was there.

KAITLIN CORTENBACH

# *Peace*

Peace is my friend.
When we hold each other's hands
We can do magic.
    My friend Peace
        was born in the heart
of the first rainbow ever.
    You can't see Peace
        but you can feel her.
Peace lives in your heart.
    Try to find her.

# *Peace Paz*

Smile! Sonrie
Be Happy! Se Féliz!
Have Fun. Diviértate.
Be Together. Siempre
esten juntos.
Play! Juga!
Always have peace.
Siempre tengan Paz.
Never think of war,
only think of peace.
Nunca pienses en la
guerra, solo en la Paz!

SARAH BARKLEY

# *Peace*

Hand in hand we walk
together
Peace and I
and
all races
black, white
and
all the
whales waltzing in the sea
all the
dolphins surfing in the splash
Hand in hand
we walk
together
and wonder
why war
why anger
why hate?
Peace and I
and all the
creatures of the
earth
together forever
Walking hand in hand.

CARA SADEL

# *Peace in the Earth*

Peace is like the hand of a mother
that heals your wounds.

Peace is a garden of blooming rainbows
ready to unite

Peace is a never ending friendship
on the earth.

Peace is what gives the earth hope.
Peace is a dolphin that swims
down a river.

Peace is what the world needs most.

CARRIE TOMLINSON

# The Flowers of the Spring

The petals fall from the flower
now to the ground.

More flowers grow.
The sun shines on the flowers
and more flowers
grow
    and

        grow.

This special purple flower
makes the moon sparkle
    and the stars
        and the planets.

When people die
        flowers
fall from the sky.

KEEGAN FOSTER

# *My World*

My world is a peaceful world a
world without fighting a world with
happiness No nuclear wars no poverty
or muggings or gangs who kill over nothing
where no one is hated
or feared where animals can
live in a rain forest without
worrying about their homes getting
destroyed for lumber My world
is a peaceful world where
a kid falls asleep without even
thinking about bad things where
a kid could walk to the park alone
without worrying about being kidnapped
My world is peaceful

ALISON TRABUCCO

# *Feel the Feeling*

Feel the feeling of flying with a butterfly and all
its beauty.
Feel the feeling of whispering to a ladybug or
singing with a sparrow.
Feel the feeling of sitting and watching an
orange and purple sunset with a dark shadow
of a bird as dark as a pencil's gray streak,
swirling with freedom across the sunset.
Feel the feeling of a parrot's squawk,
a mouse's squeal,
a bird's song,
a fish's swish
and a human's love.
Feel the feeling of peace.

SKY MCLEOD

# *World Peace*

Peace is the strongest thing on Earth
But can't even pick up a crumb.
It's impossible for peace to be spread around the world
Like bread and butter.
Good couldn't be judged.
Good would turn boring,
Boring isn't peace,
Peace isn't boring.
Peace is like water
On a drizzling day
But sometimes
You wish it was pouring.

# LESSONS

BARRY SPACKS

# *The Lesson for Today*

The Roshi suggests we take a tangerine
in the palm of the hand,
feel its weight, its intimate smooth-roughness,
observe its color, color of amazement.

He says to puncture with a fingernail
the cunning floating shell
of our tangerine, release the scent
which drifts out to us like a soul
on leave from Paradise.

We will marvel then at the segments:
toes and toes of tangerine;
will take, with each bite,
the depth-charge of the color orange
for which exist no rhymes
in English.

We will be, that is,
fully aware of one tangerine.

Entirely aware of any one thing.

Imagine, then, the Aware-Ones, in their billions,

passing on from fruit in the palm of the hand

to the cancer wards;
the killing fields;
the mutilated children.

PERIE LONGO

# *A Flash; August 6, 1945*

Though my parents danced around our apartment
with a joy I had never seen until that day,
though my oldest brother threw his box of tin soldiers
out of the fourth floor window, for good, to crash
on the street below, though my mother tossed
her crisp blue, Red Cross volunteer uniform
in a pile of dirty laundry

and even though a lady on the fifth floor threw
a bolt of fuchsia florist ribbon out her window
in celebration, that unrolled like a flash of a river
before my mother's eyes, and she gathered it in chanting
"for your hair, for your hair," exhilarated
with getting something for free, I knew
something was not right.  When my father lifted me
to his shoulders as we ran down four flights
of stairs and joined the parade of thousands below
honking horns, strewing confetti, drinking and swearing

I knew nothing was free
because I had taken a candy bar once
and got quite a licking, knew a war could not be over
just like that after four years of army green parades,
marching *clack clack* and gun maneuvers *slap slap*,
knew somebody hurt somewhere because I heard
they could "take that!" and I knew what that meant.
Inside me came a well I could not reach.

"I don't know what's got into her," mother said.
"She won't even wear those fuchsia ribbons!"
Soon after, we moved to the suburbs and I played war
with myself, me born on Pearl Harbor Day,
trying to make something come out right, throw a weight
from me that took years and years, the writing
of many poems to understand war is never
one person's fault, peace is not one person's job.

DAVID KRIEGER

# The Young Men With the Guns

for Father Roy Bourgeois

*"Let those who have a voice speak for the voiceless."*

—Bishop Oscar Romero

None of it could have happened
Not the killings, the rapes, the brutality
Without the young men with the guns.
Bishop Romero saw this clearly.
*Lay down your arms*, he said.
This, the day before his assassination,
The day before they shot him at the altar.
God, forgive them, they only follow orders.
They know not what they do.

But the politicians and the generals
Know what they do
When they give their orders
To murder at the altar.
None of it could have happened
Not the killings, the rapes, the brutality
Without the politicians and the generals.
The ones who sit in dark rooms
And stuff their mouths with food
Before they give the orders.

And the people are silent.
Their mouths will not open.
They hang their heads and avert their eyes.
Of course, they are afraid
Of the young men with the guns
Who carry out the orders.
None of it could have happened
Without the people remaining silent.
The Bishop staggered, he bled, he died
But he would never be silenced.

FELICIA MARTINEZ

# Krista says, "Rigoberta Menchú is just some Guatemalan woman they wrote a book about," and I reply

Sister, Rigoberta is just a woman
just another
  María
  Calixta
  Irena
  Xuwin
who fled barefoot from her burning hut in the highland night
just another sister lover cousin mother
who left behind a brother neighbor uncle father
a bloody leg, a fleshy skull
that soldiers piss on during patrol

She's just another Maya
who trips across borders to avoid the bullet
aching to kiss her temple
when she comes home

Sister,
Do you know Calixta
who serves you burritos at the corner taquería?
Do you know María
whose son patches your leaky roof?
Do you know Irena
who stoops to pick strawberries for your summer fruit salad?
Can you read to Xuwin
the words painted on the tractor
"Made in the USA"
so she knows who uproots
her cornfields back home?

Sister,
how tight can you shut your eyes?
Will the thin layer of flesh protect you
from the barrel aimed between your brows
when you decide to wake?

MUSHA HOVE

# Each To Her Own

Have you the time to spare a thought
For a young girl far away,
whose only task today is to wash a wall?

I do not, for I must think of others less fortunate than her.
Girls who will walk ten miles today, and then carry a bucket
    of dirty water the ten miles back home.
I cannot stop to take my mind off the girls who, today,
    will be given away in marriage
to filthy, wizened old men, to pay off a family's debt.
And those who will sit at home today,
    as they watch their younger brothers run off to school,
and pray for a morning when they too will learn to read.
Would it be right for me to forget today—even for a moment—
    those orphan girls courageously raising their families alone?
Or those slender girls, nervously roaming the streets tonight,
    in the hope of earning enough money to eat this week?
Could I live with myself after ignoring the plea for money
    by a tattered pregnant girl,
her arms holding another child, because my thoughts were elsewhere?
If not I, who would remember the young girls working
    deep in the mine shafts in China,
whose small frames make them ideal for work in hard-to-reach
    places?
Or those young girls in Bangladesh who will sit and make
    the soft toys today, that will line our supermarket shelves tomorrow?

How can I find the time, when I have no memories of strange men
    bursting into my hut and opening fire?
I have no recollection of my mother's screams as metal bullets ripped
    into her body,
exposing her organs, and splattering her flesh onto my face.

Neither do I remember watching her eyes as her body slowly slid
down the wall, staining it with a large bloody smear that resembles
the shape of the lake in which she washes our pots.
I was not present when a fervent prayer that the soldiers would
neither touch me, nor drag me with them to join their ranks
was answered by a God who had seemed non-existent moments
before.

Indeed, I have not the time to think of a girl, who buried her mother
yesterday,
and whose only task today
is to wash a wall.

BETSY LINCOLN

# *Those Who Endure*

*For the Interfaith Pilgrims for Peace and Life*
*Auschwitz to Hiroshima*
*Dec. 8, 1994 to Aug. 9, 1995*

Yours is the smokeless fire
that leaves no ash,
the gift of sorrow
which burns like a flame
that cannot be quenched.

Your enemy is not hunger,
fear, nor weariness.
All those you suffered gladly
over the months and miles
of your pilgrimage.

Your enemy is ever
that hardness of heart
you watered with your tears,
as you marched across
war-ravaged lands

chanting and beating drums,
proclaiming—through cross,
menorah, and the folded hands
of monks in saffron—
the oneness of creation.

O my dears, it is you
who could save us,
you who carry the ark
of the covenant,
and bear its weight

of conscience across
the deserts of our hearts,
as though to ransom
with your beatific smiles
some human goodness.

GAYLE BRANDEIS

# *The Body Politic of Peace*

Listen.
The body is not
a battleground,
as some people
would like you
to believe.
The body knows
peace; peace, after
all, is the body's
natural state.
Think of the body
in repose, the way
muscles loosen,
breath opens up;
think of the body
in love. It knows
what to do. It is
our mind that does
not. It is our mind
that makes us feel
separate, isolated,
it is our mind
that dreams up war.
The body says no,
come back to me,
I am fragile and strong
and I connect you
to your brothers and sisters.
I connect you to the earth.

Come back to the heartbeat,
the pulse, the rhythm
we all walk to, regardless
of nation or color. Come back
to the breath—inhale, take the world
deep into your lungs; exhale,
give yourself back fully.
This is what the body says:
release the peace
that lives within your skin.

BETTINA T. BARRETT

## *How Life Is*

It goes deep
deep down and in

a lake high up
under the sky
so deep
no bottom is ever reached

the monks' voices are deep
deep in the throat chanting
the bells quick
and the clang of cymbals

this offering every morning
and every evening        prayers
sending out
the light of joy

in this moment        every
moment        these monks are
centered        bending from the hips
forward        creating
another mandala        another
circle of meaning        the symbols
going around        colors bright
thin streams of powdered marble
here        there        all the way
this offering

and I kneel beside them      I watch
I breathe in and out
this peace and compassion
this knowing held deep
inside      just being
here in the moment
how life is

NAVEEN SUNKAVALLY

# *Peace*

Peace does not come on glorious wings
with dappled feathers that dazzle the eyes,
only to head north in the winter for bluer skies.
It does not bloom in the thick green springs
when the land is rich and brown with rain,
only to wilt and drop on exhausted terrain.

It is not worn for the fashion of the times
or a cool summer soiree near the bay,
only to be stowed in patterned safes at close of the day.
It is not a fancy French word that rhymes
or the latest current in thought that flows,
only to be discarded as society grows.

Peace cannot hear the beating of its heart,
nor can it distinguish gold from tin,
black from white, and skullcap from turban.
It is not smart or pretty or even pretty smart
but stupid and ugly, hard and crystalline
as the stone-cased night that bore it blind.

It has no vision because it is the vision.

CARMEN ELLINGSWORTH

# *Declaration of Independence*

To understand the art of warfare
Remember the games of your childhood.
Remember the power
In strength and force,
How the winner was king.
Remember the justice
In sticks and stones,
How fight made right.
Remember the glory
In forts and lairs,
How passwords winnowed.

Remember the mercy
In blackmail and bribery,
How silence meant safety.
Remember the victory
In older and bigger,
How small still ruled smaller.
Then, remember that it was only a game.
And that we were only children.

RACHEL HOPE WEARY

# *Spring*

we will be safe
my mother said
in this ivory tower
above the city streets

i was seven years old
when a man was killed
just down the hall
from where we live

i saw him once
dark bright eyes
and quick movements
shot down suddenly
like a bird in flight

yellow-striped uniforms
swarmed the grounds
like hostile bees
my stomach hurt
seeing so many guns

i did not cry
but a policeman
in ordinary clothes
solemnly handed me
a chocolate rabbit

now ugly words like
*gangs drugs*
creep into the papers
while a family grieves
over the loss of a son

outside my window
the trees are waking up
and beginning to flower
as if they too remember

that spring comes
once a year
no matter what
people do to each other

# ABOUTS

Frank K. Kelly

# Barbara Mandigo Kelly:
## The Glorious Being at the Top
## Of the Stairs

In my old house there is a large painting that looms above me when I enter the front door. I see a long flight of stairs, and at the top of the stairs there is a portrait of a woman with long dark hair, leaning on a wall. She has a red ribbon in her hair, and her right hand is pressed against her cheek. She is gazing into space with a look of longing in her clear blue eyes. Her left hand rests on the wall, and on that hand she wears a gold ring—the ring I gave her when we were married in a cathedral in New York. In her eyes I see a glint of light, and I realize how glorious she is. She is a radiant being, caught by an artist who knew that she was waiting for me to come home from a war.

As I climb the stairs I am grateful for that artist, for the gifted person who put her beautiful face upon that piece of canvas, who captured her in her full bloom, and who saw the great wave of life in her, the life she gave to me and to everyone who knew her. I am glad that Laura Lake saw what a marvelous being she was—and did that portrait as a gift for her. I am glad that the painting traveled with us as we moved from place to place, and finally landed there at the top of the stairs in our two-story house in Santa Barbara—visible to the people from all parts of the world who came to visit us.

I was among the lucky men who did come home from war with unscarred bodies, who did cleave to their wives, who resumed the lovemaking from which they had been torn by the call to battle. I had thought of her when I went on board a ship in the New York harbor, when I made the long voyage across the Atlantic. I thought of her when I was among the men who landed in Normandy and went on to the liberation of Paris—a city in which she had been a student, in which she had almost starved. I thought of her when I came back across the ocean in a plane.

I found her glowing with joy, in our small apartment on a narrow street called Patchin Place, in Greenwich Village—in the very place where we had spent our brief honeymoon. She opened her arms and took me in. By her caresses, by her kisses, by her tenderness she cleansed me from many of the painful memories I had brought with me from the torn lands of Europe.

The woman who looked upon me from that painting, Barbara Mandigo Kelly, was a poet and pianist. Wherever we lived, she filled our dwelling place with the sound of music—the music of Chopin and Debussy, of Bach and Beethoven, of Mozart and Brahms and other composers who took us into the depths of agony and up to the heights of happiness. She wrote poems about all aspects of our life together—the poignant meanings of what we shared, the activities of our sons, the griefs we encountered, the triumphs we had, the torments we endured.

Many photographs were taken of her. I have many of the letters she wrote to me when I was away in the army. I have a volume of her poems, in which she expressed a wide range of her emotions. I am grateful for all of these manifestations of her glorious vitality, but the portrait conveys more of her reality, the quality of her soul, than all the other things.

The delicate curves of her face and lips, the tenderness in her eyes, bringing back to me the feeling I had when I first saw her in the home of a friend, when I knew that I wanted her to be with me as long as I lived. The artist had glimpsed the purity of her heart, the directness of her mind, the compassion and the generous kindness that flowed from her. She had all the feminine graces of a fine woman who could give and receive the fullness of love.

On the night when I first met her, I invited her to go with me to search for a needle in a haystack. I tossed that idea at her with a smile, and she responded with laughter and two questions: "How big a haystack would it be? Could we find a needle in it in a single night?" I told her that the stack might be as high as the sky and we might need a lifetime to explore it. Her eyes danced—and my heart danced too.

Our meeting occurred in Kansas City, where I had lived before I had gone to New York to work for the Associated Press. I had returned there to be the best man at my sister's wedding, and I had a single week to get to know the woman with the dancing eyes. We had two dates, two evenings together, and then I went back to New York. I spent one night pacing the floor in the hotel room I rented with a friend, Bill Kalis, and he said to me: "You'd better call her. You can't live without her." So I called her and asked her to marry me, and she didn't hesitate for more than ten seconds before she answered: "Yes. I've been waiting for you. What took you so long?"

She came to New York early in December, and we got a license, and she telephoned the Dean of the Cathedral of St. John the Divine (who had once been her pastor in Kansas City) and he agreed to perform our wedding ceremony in the St. Ambrose Chapel. She made things clear to me: "If you faint twice in that chapel, I'll pour water on you and revive you. If you faint a third time, I'll step over you and leave you lying there on the floor. I've heard that men often collapse when it's time to take a vow to live with one woman for life." I answered her crisply: "I won't collapse, darling. I know all about you. We've had two dates."

The Dean listened to our promises of deep faithfulness, and he blessed us and tied us together with a holy garment, and then he released us and sent us forth into the huge nave of that mighty cathedral. It was twilight and an organist was practicing some sacred music on a giant organ, and the music rolled over us in a tremendous wave. Hal Boyle of the Associated Press, a witness at that wedding, looked down the length of that immense building and whispered: "Isn't it a pity that Jesus didn't live to see this place or hear this music?" And someone said: "He's here."

We got in a taxi and went down to a restaurant in Greenwich Village, and we feasted. We sang and we danced and we drank champagne. Then Barbara and I walked over to Patchin Place, and we climbed the stairs to a small apartment provided by a friend who was moving to Peru.

Whenever I look at the painting of that glorious being at the top of the stairs in my house, a torrent of memories rushes through me. I remember the war years, the years of getting to know one another, the years of writing and singing and dancing in New York, the times in Cambridge when I was a Nieman Fellow at Harvard, the days when I was on the faculty at Boston University, the months when I wrote speeches for Harry Truman, my years of working for the Senate in Washington, my participation in Averell Harriman's run for the presidency, our return to New York, and then our long journey across the country to the golden land of California. In all the swings and changes of a tumultuous life, we were together.

On the second morning of our honeymoon, we felt the shadows of destruction and death. We were listening to the New York Philharmonic orchestra, submerged in the music that poured from a small radio near our bed. For us, music was always the food of love. I held her in my arms, and our hearts were beating together. Suddenly the music stopped and a man's voice went through us like a sword: "Japanese planes have bombed Pearl Harbor." We broke apart and we cried out the name of God, the God who had blessed us in the cathedral, and I said: "We don't have to be in it. We didn't bring it on." But Barbara said: "We are in it. But it won't destroy us. We'll get through it. Nothing can destroy what we have."

And we did get through it. I was taken into the army, I escaped death when a Nazi torpedo hit a ship close to me while crossing the Atlantic, I survived air raids in England, I landed in France unwounded, I took part in the liberation of Paris, and I came back to New York in 1945 after the victory in Europe, full of passion, eager to sweep her into my arms again. I knew there was a chance I might be sent to the Pacific, where the fighting was still furious. We decided to have a child, a lasting sign of our joining together, a sign of our faith in the future, a being born of our blending of bodies and souls, a child who would have the best qualities of both of us and many special gifts beyond our imagining. We were prepared to welcome a daughter or son with equal thanksgiving.

President Truman ordered the atomic bombing of two Japanese cities, and the Japanese surrendered more swiftly than we had expected. I wasn't sent to the Pacific, but we did have a child—a son bursting with energy, eager to explore everything, handsome and brilliant, with an enormous zest for life and a huge determination to overcome all frustrations and limitations. He astounded us in every stage of his development and made us realize that we needed a flood of God's grace to meet the challenges he presented to us. We loved him and admired him, but our wisdom was not sufficient to do him justice.

When our second son came, we were again stretched to our limits. Like his brother, he had a wide range of gifts. He was awed by his brother, who was bigger and stronger than he was. He had particular abilities as a musician, as a mathematician, and as did his brother, he often contemplated the glorious being depicted in the painting. That portrait helped him—as it helped his brother—to understand the beauty and the loving spirit of his poet mother.

Whenever I look at it now, I remember her dancing eyes and the glow of light I saw around her when she was introduced to me. I remember the whisper that came to me: "That's the darling girl you've been seeking." And she was indeed the right one—my bride, my counselor, my companion, my treasure, my critic, and my comforter. She played with me and scolded me, she cooked for me and fed me, she advised me when I had to make hard decisions, she soared with me and fell with me, she was with me when I was feeling wild and happy, she was there when I was sick and I was sad, she assured me that wonderful opportunities would come to me. She always told the truth, I trusted her completely, and she never let me down. When we had fights, she was quick to be the peacemaker. She was full of forgiveness—and I needed it often.

We had 54 years together before she departed from this life.

Whenever I climb the steps in our house, I have a feeling that she is with me. I look up—and raise my right hand toward the beautiful woman above me, the Glorious Being at the top of the stairs.

# ABOUT TERRY TEMPEST WILLIAMS

TERRY TEMPEST WILLIAMS, a fifth-generation Mormon, grew up within sight of the Great Salt Lake in Salt Lake City, Utah. Her ancestors followed Brigham Young, "the American Moses," to the Promised Land for spiritual sovereignty in 1847, fleeing the prosecutions they met in Navhoo, Illinois, after the murder of their prophet, Joseph Smith.

"I write through my biases of gender, geography, and culture. I am a woman whose ideas have been shaped by the Great Basin and Colorado Plateau. These ideas are then filtered through the prism of my culture, and my culture is Mormon. These tenets of family and community, which I see at the heart of that culture, are then articulated through story."

Williams is perhaps best known for her book *Refuge: An Unnatural History of Family and Place* (Pantheon, 1991), in which she chronicles the epic rise of the Great Salt Lake and the flooding of the Bear River Migratory Bird Refuge in 1983 (alongside her mother's diagnosis of ovarian cancer, believed to have been caused by radioactive fallout from nuclear tests in the Nevada desert in the 1950s and 1960s) and which is now regarded as a classic in American Nature Writing, a testament to loss and the earth's healing grace. The *San Francisco Chronicle* wrote, "There has never been a book like *Refuge.* . . . utterly original."

Her other books include *Red: Passion and Patience in the Desert* (Pantheon, 2001); *Leap* (Pantheon, 2000/Vintage, 2001); *An Unspoken Hunger* (Pantheon, 1994); *Desert Quartet: An Erotic Landscape* (Pantheon, 1995); *Coyote's Canyon* (Gibbs M. Smith, 1989); and *Pieces of White Shell: A Journey to Navajoland* (Charles Scribner and Sons, 1984). She is also the author of two children's books: *The Secret Language of Snow* (Sierra Club/Pantheon, 1984); and *Between Cattails* (Little Brown, 1985).

Her work has been widely anthologized, having also appeared in *The*

*New Yorker, The Nation, Outside, Audubon, Orion, The Iowa Review*, and *The New England Review*, among other national and international publications.

Williams was identified by *Newsweek* in 1991 as someone likely to make "a considerable impact on the political, economic, and environmental issues facing the western states this decade." She has served on the Governing Council of the Wilderness Society and was a member of the western team for the President's Council for Sustainable Development. She is currently on the advisory board of the National Parks and Conservation Association, The Nature Conservancy, and the Southern Utah Wilderness Alliance.

She has testified before the United States Congress twice regarding issues of women's health and the environmental links associated with cancer and has been a strong advocate for America's Redrock Wilderness Act, protecting the redrock canyons of southern Utah.

As one of the editors of *Testimony: Writers Speak On Behalf of Utah Wilderness*, she organized twenty American writers to pen their thoughts on why the protection of these wildlands matters. When President Clinton dedicated the new Grand Staircase-Escalante National Monument on September 18, 1996, he held up this book on the North Rim of the Grand Canyon and said, "This made a difference."

She was recently inducted to the Rachel Carson Honor Roll and has received the National Wildlife Federation's Conservation Award for Special Achievement.

*The Utne Reader* named Terry Tempest Williams as one of their "Utne 100 Visionaries," in their words, "a person who could change your life."

She has been a fellow for the John Simon Guggenheim Memorial Foundation and received a Lannan Literary Fellowship in Creative Nonfiction.

In 1999, Ms. Williams received "The Spirit of the West" award from the Mountain-Plains Booksellers Association for Special Literary Achievement. She has also been recognized by the Mormon Arts & Letters Association and honored by Physicians for Social Responsibility for "distinguished contributions in literature, ecology, and advocacy for an environmentally sustainable world."

Formerly naturalist-in-residence at the Utah Museum of Natural History, Ms. Williams now lives in Castle Valley, Utah, with her husband, Brooke Williams.

# ABOUT DAVID KRIEGER

DAVID KRIEGER is a founder of the Nuclear Age Peace Foundation and has served as President of the Foundation since 1982. Under his leadership the Foundation has initiated many innovative and important projects for building peace, strengthening international law, and abolishing nuclear weapons. Dr. Krieger has lectured throughout the United States, Europe, and Asia on issues of peace, security, international law, and the abolition of nuclear weapons. He has been interviewed on CNN Hotline, MSNBC, and many other television and radio shows nationally and internationally.

Dr. Krieger is the author of many studies of peace in the Nuclear Age. Among the books he has written or edited are *Choose Hope, Your Role in Waging Peace in the Nuclear Age; Nuclear Weapons and the World Court; A Maginot Line in the Sky: International Perspectives on Ballistic Missile Defense; Disarmament and Development: The Challenge of the International Control and Management of Dual-Purpose Technologies; Waging Peace in the Nuclear Age, Ideas for Action; Waging Peace II, Vision and Hope for the 21st Century;* and *The Tides of Change: Peace, Pollution and Potential of the Oceans.*

Dr. Krieger is a board member of the Lawyers Committee on Nuclear Policy (New York), deputy chair of the International Network of Engineers and Scientists for Global Responsibility (Germany), a member of the Committee of 100 for Tibet, and a member of the International Steering Committee of the Middle Powers Initiative. He is also a founder of Abolition 2000, a global network of over 2000 organizations and municipalities committed to the elimination of nuclear weapons.

He serves on the Advisory Council of Free the Children International (Toronto), Global Resource Action Center for the Environment (New

York), the International Council of the Institute on the Holocaust and Genocide (Israel), the International Institute for Peace (Vienna), the Peace Resources Cooperative (Japan), the Transnational Foundation for Peace and Future Research (Sweden), and the War and Peace Foundation (New York).

He is a recipient of the Bronze Medal of the Hungarian Engineers for Peace (1995); the Peace Award of the War and Peace Foundation (1996); the Big Canvas Award of Santa Barbara Magazine (1996); the Soka Gakkai International Peace and Culture Award (1997); the Soka University Award of Highest Honor (1997); the Soka Gakkai Hiroshima Peace Award (2000); the Peace Award of the International Journal of Humanities and Peace (2000); the Peace Educator of the Year Award of the Consortium of Peace Research, Education and Development (2001); and the Gakudo Peace Award of the Ozaki Yukio Memorial Foundation (2001).

He is a graduate of Occidental College and holds M.A. and Ph.D. degrees in political science from the University of Hawaii as well as a J.D. from the Santa Barbara College of Law.

Dr. Krieger lives in Santa Barbara, California. He is married and has three children. His interests include tennis, hiking, and poetry.

# ABOUT THE JUDGES

**Bettina T. Barrett**, born and raised in Denmark, began writing poetry as a teenager. She has published three books of poetry, *Bear-Star My Name, Sleepdancer* and *Heartscape.*

**Susan Miles Gulbransen** is a freelance writer, former columnist for the *Santa Barbara News-Press*, writing teacher, co-director of the Annual Santa Barbara Book & Author Festival, and community volunteer.

**Gene Knudsen Hoffman** is a poet, poetry teacher and peace worker. She is the author of many books, including *All Possible Surprises* (1991), a collection of poetry. She is a former chair of the Nuclear Age Peace Foundation Poetry Committee.

**Perie Longo** is the author of two poetry books, *Milking the Earth* (1986) and *The Privacy of Wind* (1997). She is on the staff of the Santa Barbara Writers Conference, teaches poetry writing through California-Poets-in-the-Schools and is a psychotherapist in private practice who uses poetry for healing. She is the chair of the Nuclear Age Peace Foundation Poetry Committee.

**Glenna Luschei** was made Poet Laureate of San Luis Obispo in 2000. She is the publisher of *Solo* and *Café Solo* magazines. She has published twenty books of poetry, including, most recently *Shot with Eros* (2002).

**Sojourner Kincaid Rolle** is a poet, poetry advocate and mediator. She is the author of five chapbooks of poetry, including *Common Ancestry* (1999).

**Barry Spacks** is a visiting professor at the University of California at Santa Barbara. He has published two novels and seven poetry collections, including *Brief Sparrow* and *Spacks Street: New and Selected Poems.*

**Chryss Yost** is co-editing a comprehensive overview of California poetry. Her poems have been published internationally and are in several anthologies, including *Introduction to Poetry* (2002) and *The Geography of Home: California's Poetry of Place* (1999).

# ABOUT THE BARBARA MANDIGO KELLY
## PEACE POETRY AWARDS

The Barbara Mandigo Kelly Peace Poetry Awards are an annual series of awards created by the Nuclear Age Peace Foundation to encourage poets to explore and illuminate positive visions of peace and the human spirit. Open to people worldwide, the contest has been held each year since 1996. The contest honors the late Barbara Mandigo Kelly, a Santa Barbara poet and longtime supporter of peace issues. Frank Kelly, who was her husband, is a founding member of the Foundation and serves as its Senior Vice-President.

For more information and to view the current Barbara Mandigo Kelly Peace Poetry Awards guidelines, please visit the Foundation's website at www.wagingpeace.org/new/programs/awardscontests/bmk/index.htm or write to the Foundation at:

> Barbara Mandigo Kelly Peace Poetry Awards
> Nuclear Age Peace Foundation
> PMB 121, 1187 Coast Village Road, Suite 1
> Santa Barbara, California  93108-2794

# ABOUT THE NUCLEAR AGE PEACE FOUNDATION

The Nuclear Age Peace Foundation's vision is a world at peace, free of the threat of war and free of weapons of mass destruction. The Foundation's mission is to advance initiatives to eliminate the threat of nuclear weapons to all life, to foster the global rule of law, and to build an enduring legacy of peace through education and advocacy.

Founded in 1982, the Nuclear Age Peace Foundation (NAPF) is a non-profit, non-partisan, international education and advocacy organization. In 2002, the Foundation celebrates twenty years of service to the local, national and international communities.

The Foundation initiates and supports worldwide efforts to abolish nuclear weapons, to strengthen international law and institutions, to use technology responsibly and sustainably, and to empower young people to create a more peaceful world.

For more information on the Nuclear Age Peace Foundation, it programs, and how to get involved, visit the Foundation's principal website at

## www.wagingpeace.org

We also encourage you to visit the following Foundation websites:

| | |
|---|---|
| Nuclear Files | www.nuclearfiles.org |
| Moving Beyond Missile Defense | www.mbmd.org |
| UC Nuclear Free | www.ucnuclearfree.org |
| End of Existence | www.endofexistence.org |

# INDEXES

# INDEX OF POEMS

# INDEX OF AUTHORS

Cortenbach, Kaitlin, *Peace*
    2000, 1st Place, 12 and Under Category

Crafton, Sylvia, *the peacemaker*
    1998, Honorable Mention, 13-18 Years Old Category

Crewse, Roselyn, *The Sound of Peace*
    1996, Honorable Mention, Adult Category

Durkin, Rebecca, *A Night to Travel*
    2001, Honorable Mention, 13-18 Years Old Category

Ellingsworth, Carmen, *Declaration of Independence*
    2001, 1st Place, 13-18 Years Old Category

Foster, Keegan, *My World*
    1996, Honorable Mention, 12 and Under Category

Gebhardt, Bear Jack, *On Allard St*
    1996, Honorable Mention, Adult Category

Gulbransen, Susan Miles, *The Intruders*
    BMK Poetry Awards Judge

Gluck, Marlee J., *Peace*
    2001, Honorable Mention, 12 and Under Category

Hamdani, Sasha G., *I Want to Touch the World*
    1997, 1st Place, 12 and Under Category,

Hartman, Jeffrey, *Ode to the Swans*
    1999, Honorable Mention, 12 and Under Category

Hoffman, Gene Knudsen, *I am Waiting*
    BMK Poetry Awards Judge

Hove, Musha, *Each to Her Own*
    2002, 1st Place, 13-18 Years Old Category

Kass, Bryn, *What is Peace*
   2000, Honorable Mention, 12 and Under Category

Kelly, Barbara Mandigo, *For the Year of Peril, 1942*

Krieger, David, *Dance of Hiroshima*
   *The Young Men With the Guns*
   President, Nuclear Age Peace Foundation

Kovacik, Karen, *Requiem for the Buddhas of Bamiyan*
   2002, 1st Place, Adult Category

Lane, J. Keiko, *Winter Tomatoes*
   1998, 1st Place, Adult Category

Lapp, Claudia, *Lake*
   1996, 1st Place, Adult Category

Lincoln, Betsy, *Those Who Endure*
   1998, Honorable Mention, Adult Category

Longo, Perry, *A Flash; August 6, 1945*
   BMK Poetry Awards Judge

Luschei, Glenna, *Peace in the Forest*
   BMK Poetry Awards Judge

Martinez, Felicia, *Krista says, "Rigoberta Menchú is just some*
   *Guatemalan woman they wrote a book about," and I reply*
   2002, Honorable Mention, Adult Category

Mason, Keith Antar, *lovers on ground zero*
   1997, 1st Place, Adult Category

McGarry, Susan Lloyd, *Washing*
   2002, Honorable Mention, Adult Category

McLeod, Sky, *World Peace*
    2002, 1st Place, 12 and Under Category

Moses, Marina, *Theseus Slaying the Minotaur, a Sculpture by
    Antoine-Louise Barye*
    2000, Honorable Mention, 13-18 Years Old Category

Moses, Marina, *This Is My Fear*
    1999, Honorable Mention, 13-18 Years Old Category

Murphy, Kett, *What is Peace*
    1997, Honorable Mention, 13-18 Years Old Category

Nagata, Jonathan, *Forced from Home*
    1999, 1st Place, 12 and Under Category

Nikko, *atomic garden*
    2000, 1st Place, Adult Category

Nunziata, Will, *Gramma*
    2002, Honorable Mention, 13-18 Years Old Category

Parvin, Debbie, *Peacemaker*
    1996, Honorable Mention, Adult Category

Ray, David, *Flying Over Cheyenne Mountain*
    2001, 1st Place, Adult Category

Rider, Amy, *Nagasaki Trees*
    2002, Honorable Mention, 13-18 Years Old Category

Rolle, Sojourner Kincaid, *Where the Hum Begins*
    BMK Poetry Awards Judge

Rubinstein, Cara, *The Peace of the Night,*
    1997, Honorable Mention, 12 and Under Category

Russell, Anthony, *After Vespers at the Monastery, Abiquiu, NM,*
    2000, Honorable Mention, Adult Category

Sadel, Cara, *Peace in the Earth*
    1998, Honorable Mention, 12 and Under Category

Schneider, Gavin, *Sacred Dust*
    2001, 1st Place, 12 and Under Category

Segal, Jess, *signs of peace?*
    1996, Honorable Mention, 13-18 Years Old Category

Shipley, Vivian C., *Digging Up Peonies*
    1999, Honorable Mention, Adult Category

Spacks, Barry, *The Lesson for Today*
    BMK Poetry Awards Judge

Stempeck, Brian, *a moment of faith*
    1996, 1st Place, 13-18 Years Old Category

Steury, Alec, *Chinese Moon*
    2000, 1st Place, 13-18 Years Old Category

Sunkavally, Naveen, *Peace*
    1997, 1st Place, 13-18 Years Old Category

Tomlinson, Carrie, *The Flowers of the Spring*
    1996, Honorable Mention, 12 and Under Category

Trabucco, Alison, *Feel the Feeling*
    1996, 1st Place, 12 and Under Category

Traicoff, Kristin, *Clouds*
    1996, Honorable Mention, 13-18 Years Old Category

Turner, Heather, *Peace Defined*
    1996, Honorable Mention, 13-18 Years Old Category

Vizzo, Emily, *Untitled*
    1998, 1st Place, 13-18 Years Old Category

von Hoffman, Kristen, *Happy*
  1999, 1st Place, 13-18 Years Old Category

Weary, Rachel Hope, *September 11*
  2002, Honorable Mention, 12 and Under Category

Weary, Rachel Hope, *Spring*
  2002, Honorable Mention, 12 and Under Category

Whitehead, Gary J., *Arboretum*
  1997, Honorable Mention, Adult Category

Wilson, Evanne, *Sunflower*
  1996, Honorable Mention, 12 and Under Category,

Wilson, Marina, *Poem for MJ Polo*
  2001, Honorable Mention, Adult Category

Yost, Chryss, *Graduation Day*
  BMK Poetry Awards Judge

Two thousand two hundred copies of *The Poetry of Peace* were printed by Capra Press in October 2002. In addition, one hundred copies have been numbered and signed by Mr. Krieger and Ms. Williams. Twenty-six copies in slipcases were also lettered and signed by both.

Bird O
Gargus
time
Korth Brok

zygon
O2O

the luminous Shadow